"Hearty, glad praise for *Neither Created Nor Destroyed*, 2012 Philbrick Poetry Project Honoree. The reader should prepare for a bit of a journey led by a poet comfortable in many realms: the natural world, family, education, and work appear and reappear in this collection, and through the poet's unique blend of sensitivity and language, these seemingly familiar themes become transformed. These are textured poems, some as ruddy as the old farmer who peoples one of them, and others as comforting as 'waves' that 'break like heartbeats.' Lucile Burt knows the mind and heart of surf-caster and sullen schoolgirl alike; she understands the difficulties of love, the beautiful pain of caring for an elderly parent, and the wisdom of the riverbed, and through these poems, delivers 'the riotous chorus of matter' to us freshly washed and brand new."

— Lisa Starr

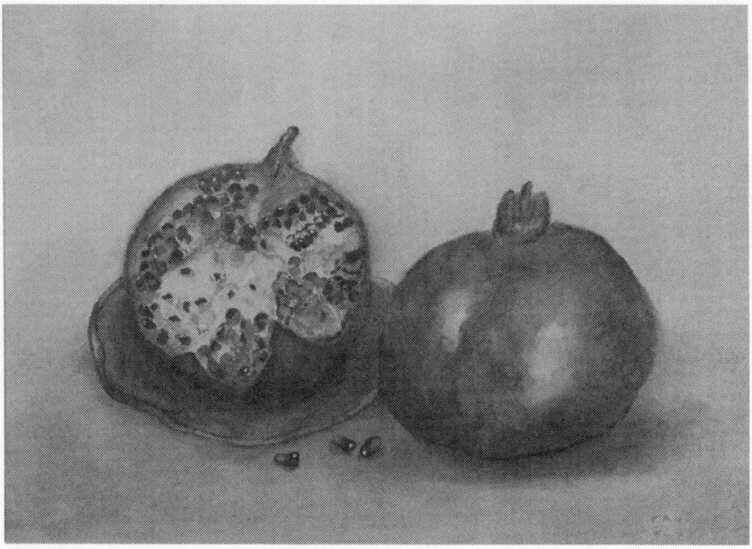

NEITHER CREATED NOR DESTROYED

POEMS BY
LUCILE BURT

*Lucile Burt
for Aoiha
Block Island
April 2015*

THE PROVIDENCE ATHENAEUM
Providence, Rhode Island

Copyright 2012 by Lucile Burt
All Rights Reserved

ISBN 0-922558-65-5

Published in cooperation with The Poet's Press

Cover art by Phyllis Kutt

This chapbook is published by The Providence Athenaeum as part of the Philbrick Poetry Project, established in 1998 to honor the memory of Charles and Deborah Philbrick. The Philbrick Poetry Project honors an outstanding, emerging New England poet who has not yet published a book. Lisa Starr selected *Neither Created Nor Destroyed*.

Partial support for this project was provided by the Philbrick Family and by donations to the Philbrick Poetry Project Fund.

Generous funding was also provided by a grant from the Rhode Island State Council on the Arts, through an appropriation by the Rhode Island General Assembly and a grant from the National Endowment for the Arts.

RISCA
Art is the Anchor

CONTENTS

Saving the Turtles 13
At the Saturday Market, Sapa, Viet Nam 14
Senior English: Reading Shakespeare 15
Bad Boys 16
Dreaming the River 17
Someone Loved Returning 19
Autumn Equinox, Duck Pond 20
Night Walk 21
Melissa Quits School 22
The Last Journey 24
Surfcasting 25
March Light 27
Sleeping at the Beach 28
Stroke 29
Neither Created Nor Destroyed 30
New Moon in Bali 32
What They Feared 33
Eve's Story 34
Darwin Waterstraw 36
Matisse's *Icarus* 38
Writers' Retreat 39

About the Poet 40
Acknowledgments 41

for Phyllis Kutt
1947-2012

Friend, our closeness is this:
Anywhere you put your foot, feel me
in the firmness under you.
— RUMI

NEITHER CREATED
NOR DESTROYED

SAVING THE TURTLES

for my father

When I could not save your life,
I saved instead box turtles
and endangered terrapins,
who, driven by instinct
to the egg-laying place,
ventured onto risky pavement.

When I gathered them in my hands,
gingerly, to avoid a nip,
they retreated in their shells, not knowing
with what gratitude my hands
lifted them to the other side.

At home, the nurse's hands,
more sure than mine,
ministered to your final needs,
turning you, massaging your heels,
combing your hair, even though
you had retreated inside, your eyes
fixed on something beyond the ceiling.

You were so light, your skin
a thin covering for bone, that I imagined
I could lift you, light as a turtle,
carry you safely to the other side.

AT THE SATURDAY MARKET, SAPA, VIET NAM

Red Dao women stream
into town on a river of color,
festooned with flounces and ribbons,
hair combs and folderol.

Old women latch on like crabs
to tourists caught in the market's eddies.
"How much you pay?" they thrust
their crafts into stunned faces.

In the whirlpools, young women dance
the universal mating dance: lifted petticoats,
flashing teeth and eyes, whispers, giggles,
glances held a beat too long.

Boys, stunned witless, circle the bait.
Those brash beauties do not look down
the short path where this dance ends,
visible only a few feet away,

the shapeless mothers and grandmothers,
bent by firewood on backs, babies in bellies,
fingers stained by indigo dye.
Those women know

this dance women have danced
for centuries, all heat and innocence,
this trap of beauty, the heady power,
that, for an instant, holds the world in thrall.

SENIOR ENGLISH: READING SHAKESPEARE

She reads some crazy words and then she stops.
She has to tell the meaning of each line.
I hate the stopping. It's her voice I want,
the beat of words. She taught the name to us,
but I forget. We counted syllables
and I was bored. But when she only reads
and stops explaining every single word,
and doesn't count the syllables at all,
and doesn't ask for answers I don't know,
I let my ears blur out the words she reads,
and hardly think but anchor to her voice,
a boat that floats on iambs (*that's* the name)
that's rocking on a rhythm like the sea.
I cut the rope and let my boat drift free.

BAD BOYS

uniformed in black
pack the back of the bus.
Voices, staccato as jackhammers,
brag of conquests, grand and alarming:
girl-charming, beer-swilling, punch-wielding lies.
Boots on the seats, they thump the rhythm
of ear blasting bass from personal stereos.
They speak the clipped clichés
of clipped imaginations.

At the end of the line, bad boys
bolt from the bus, harass
nice girls and boys in hissing whispers:
faggot. slut.
Hunched over last cigarettes, they stand
like a murder of lean crows,
wary, easily spooked.
They might, at any moment,
take flight in a raucous chorus,
shrink to dark specks,
disappear.

DREAMING THE RIVER

I come up through layers of sleep
to find you propped on an elbow
staring down at me, puzzled.
"What are you doing in the river?"
"Wake up," I say. "You're dreaming."

The current tugs as you stand
knee-deep in the Cowlitz or Kalamah,
peering into water too clear for fishing.
They can see you; they know
what you have come for.

And you can see them,
steelhead, sleek and muscular,
hugging shady banks and rock shadows.
They are still in mid-summer heat.
They will not rise.

Two weeks you have fished, day and night.
You cast in mesmerizing rhythm,
land flies delicately on the current,
trying to tease just one fish to rise.
The rivers have entered your dreams.

Now, in the dark, half-awakened,
when I cannot pull you back from the river,
I give in to the current of your dream.
Sun glares off the surface
as I slide into cool green water.

From below I see you
staring down, willing me to rise,
a shimmering fish
driven by hunger, or curiosity,
or the sheer strength of your will.

Around me, silver bellies of steelhead
glint in and out of sunlight.
I glide into shadows
in cool stillness at the bottom.
I will not rise.

SOMEONE LOVED RETURNING

Even if all those we ever loved,
leaving, went lightly,
and we knew they would return,

even if we recognized them when they came
as hurricanes or cardinals,
and we could speak
the language of weather and birds,

even if we had the patience to wait,
listening, and let them come
in their own ways,
however terrifying or trivial,

and when they came, we forgave
history and old hurts, willing
to hear their songs or howling,

even if we knew we ourselves
would return as reeds or beetles,
forgiven for our whispers and hunger,

even if we saw in every tremor,
every saxophone wail,
every stone rolled by waves at our feet,
someone loved returning,

would you and I, now,
meet like the horizon at twilight,
dark and open, edges blurring?

AUTUMN EQUINOX, DUCK POND

I stand waist deep while ripples settle.
So still that dragonflies dance close, dart away.
A thin mist hovers like a lethargic ghost.
Scrub pine and oak, waning half moon,
cloudless sky all shimmer on the pond surface.

On this day of equal dark and light,
I stand in windless equilibrium
where temperatures of air and water meet,
where the world above is the world below,
and I am half in each.

NIGHT WALK

I walk home under a sad sky.
The light is so luminous
around the street lamps
and the rain-wet street,
I imagine I might find you
wandering in the mist.

I cannot forgive the lies.
But I might listen to another
if it shines like these lamps.

MELISSA QUITS SCHOOL

I'm not going down into that cave anymore,
that room *under* everything
where they stick us freaks
surrounded by storage rooms
and a hundred years of dust
caking little windows near the ceiling.

We're buried under the weight
of all those rooms above us,
regular rooms with regular kids,
buried where we won't be a bad influence.

Mrs. Miller says I'll be sorry,
but I don't care. I can't think
down there. It's hard to breathe
underground.
If school's so great for my future,
what's Mrs. Miller doing down here
like some sad dead bird
teaching us freaks
and smelling like booze every morning?

I may be stupid, but I know this:
outside there'll be light and air
and I won't feel like I'm dying.
Outside, someone will pay when I work,
give me a coffee break when I can smoke.
No one will say "where's your pass?"
Sandy and Tina won't dance away from me,
sidestepping like I'm poison ivy,
and boys won't try to pry me open.

Steve won't be hanging on me,
wanting me
to take a couple of hits before class,
wanting me
to cut class to make love,
even though it's really screwing
and he calls it "making love"
so I'll do it and he can brag later.

I may be stupid, but I know this:
even just a little light and air
can save your life.
That shark Steve thinks he owns me,
but I know this:
when we cruise in his car
so he can show off his Chevy and me
him looking out the window all the time,
going nowhere, just cruising,
I'm there 'cause we're moving,
I'm there alone with Tori Amos,
singing her sad true songs,
leaning my head back,
watching the streetlights come and go,
each flash lighting my face
for a minute in the dark.

THE LAST JOURNEY

I took with my father
was a scenic ride
on the Cape Cod Railroad
from Hyannis to the canal
and back. The scenery,
a tangled wall of brambles
gave way sometimes
for a glimpse
of cranberry bog or salt marsh.

This line is all that's left.
No train travels
all the way to Provincetown.
That former rail bed
is a bike path now
or a ghost trail
nearly buried in woods.

Few people rode that day.
We sat alone in a car,
my father content on that train
with no destination.
We spoke of ordinary things,
dozed to the rhythmic rocking.
Time passed as always,
a tangled blur that opens
briefly to the long view.

SURFCASTING

Solitary men in waders
line the shore at first light.
The sea is a dappled purple.
They are watching for signs:
the churn of baitfish,
the cacophonous swirl of gulls.
They are thinking of fish,
not women.

They cast with the whole arc of body.
The weighted line carries
the barbed question mark
out into deep water.
No one wants the easy answers:
flat rippling wings of skate,
tangle of rubbery sea ribbon,
even the bluefish, so voracious
it will strike anything.

The men wait with the patience of herons,
or the restless circling of terns.
They are willing to go away empty
unless they can land the splendid,
wily prize, the striped bass
whose hard strike bows the rod,
whose fight arcs it high out of the water,
where it dances for a moment on air,
a gray and silver shimmer,
a leap of shining muscle.

These are not grizzled fishermen
chugging out at night in trawlers
to Stellwagen Bank, where in deep water
their nets will gather so many fish
that none surprises. This is sport,
not livelihood, a story
about luck and the right lure,
rod bent at the strike, the fight.

Once the fish is landed,
they are indifferent.
They can send it back, take it home,
either way.

MARCH LIGHT

Cambridge, Massachusetts

You slept. I watched
afternoon light
the color of Spanish summer,
slant over your turned back,
shimmer on the painting
of whitewashed houses
against Andalusian sky.

March light dazzled,
pretending heat,
as if we might lie
like someone in that village
dozing in the thick hour of siesta.

For a few hours, light
blazed bright on those houses.
Now a different slant
leaves us in shadows,
in cool blue silence.

SLEEPING AT THE BEACH

We are hypnotized by the flash of sun
on the hammered medallion of the sea.
Heavy-lidded, we surrender.
Noon sun turns the dozing world crimson.
The whine of one fly grows close,

becomes the engine whine of a plane
careening out of the nightmare sunfire.
Bomb doors open; whistling shells
fall in slow motion, growing huge.
I hold my breath, wondering
how they will separate our parts for burial.

I come awake like a whip crack,
watch the dream retreat,
focus on the thin membrane
at the base of your throat
where heartbeat is always visible.

STROKE

No longer impatient for death, has she learned
that death can't be hurried?   Or perhaps the notion of hurry
is only for those who know the passing of hours.
She waits for death to arrive, not with fanfare,
but with a sudden lift to a place where it all stops.

How did it begin, this slush of words and time?
With a small pop like a pulled cork?
Or a slight shift, like a sparrow wing, at the core?
What is it like inside her mind?   Hours collapsing,
expanding, not measured by a clock, but by the wild flux
of her life rambling over eight decades.

In the tangle, my arrival pulls a thread to lucidity.
I bring talismans, her mother's cameo,
a necklace of cowry shells my father made her,
old photographs.   She barely looks at them.
She is casting off all that tethers her.
I know that I am next, now or next year.
I grip the last line tight as she grows lighter.

NEITHER CREATED NOR DESTROYED

Think of the air then.
Think of atoms from a burned
beeswax candle lifted by heat
into air, atoms that were once
nectar, and before that, bud, stalk,
root, seed, all that grew from life
decomposed, whisked off on wind.

I buried only half
of my parents' co-mingled ashes.
The rest I saved for the garden.
I left them unburied for years,
inert in their urn. They nagged,
not for burial, but
the untended garden.

Their atomized hearts and lungs
were already gone on the currents,
rained on the ocean perhaps, or
a London street or a field in China,
turned to hurricane, run-off, rice.

Finally, November, I pull up
overgrown grass and weed. I turn
over earth and memory.
Here grew food for the summer table.
Over the raw earth, I scatter their ashes,
dig them down to root depth
where they wait all winter.

In June, no practical plants
rise from their bones.
Instead, the last of them blooms
into poppy, snapdragon, daisy,
into coreopsis, columbine, cosmos,
the riotous chorus of matter.

NEW MOON IN BALI

Air thick and moist as breath.
No sound but susurrus of surf.
The dark moon tugs the tide.
Absent, she opens the night
to smaller light. Stars,
luminescent plankton,
fireflies, fishermen's lanterns
glitter on all sides,
above and underfoot.

I step into the starry sea.
My body, moon-pulled,
plankton-lit, rocks
on the moon-pulled surf.
Waves break like heartbeats,
roll back sighing.
I float in the womb night,
waiting.

WHAT THEY FEARED

Don't throw a leg
over the back of a horse
and gallop.
You might burst your hymen.

Don't wrap your legs
around the belly
of a djembe.
You might fry your eggs.

Ride like a lady.
Drum like a lady.
Sidesaddle.
Keep your knees together.

When a woman rides
bareback, wind whipping her
hair, the hard muscle
of horse surges beneath her.

When she holds a djembe
tight between her thighs,
her hands on the head
thrum the root chakra.

Oh yes, oh yes yes,
this is what they feared.

EVE'S STORY

In the beginning, in the garden
in the sun's afternoon warmth,
Eve dozed beneath an apple tree,
cool in dappled shade.

A movement, a small shift
inside her head, like an eyelash,
turned her vision in.
She felt a second heart,

a slow reptilian beat, and the shape
of something stirring. She heard
her own voice, a strange echo
turned inside: "Who are you?"

In the eternal stillness of the garden,
in the tranquil present filled
with apples perpetually ripe,
Eve heard the whispered answer:

"Serpent," a voice dry as leaves,
stealthy as thought.
And Eve spoke again:
"What are you doing there?"

And Serpent replied,
"I live here."
"Isn't it cramped?"
"No, I'm a metaphor."

Serpent saw that Eve
was puzzled by these words
that slithered at the edge
and made her tremble.

When Serpent spoke again
in a sibilant voice like wind
that shook the tree so apples fell,
Eve took one in her hand.

Then Serpent went still,
curled inside Eve's darkness,
listening for the sound
of teeth tearing skin.

DARWIN WATERSTRAW

In the field behind our house the tractor circled.
Restless, restricted to our yard for days,
we watched the farmer Darwin Waterstraw
plough then plant then harvest crops of hay.
Each time he passed, we waved.
Tanned and taciturn, he waved back.

He worked his way around the field and back,
the droning tractor making ever-smaller circles.
Midday heat rose from the earth in waves,
and we waited for the passing of these days
for the time when Darwin's thriving hay
grew tall and turned from green to straw.

Then we flattened out the stalks like straw
to make a narrow trail that doubled back
around, a winding path of ruined hay.
Hidden in the maze, we made a circle
where I would sometimes lie for half a day
and watch the stalks above me toss and wave.

In the womb of hay, I dozed and woke in waves.
Long afternoons smelled of heat and earth and straw.
I never counted summer's time or days
except to know that Darwin would come back.
In the constant plant and harvest circle,
he'd come one day to cut the hay.

We feared he'd scold about the hay,
but he said nothing, only waved
his silent greeting from each slow circle.
Though we were grateful for Waterstraw's
forbearance, we'd still sneak back
when hay grew tall again in shortening days.

On the last hot harvest days,
when he and helpers bucked the bales of hay,
my father'd offer him a beer. He'd slug it back,
pull off his hat, wipe the sweat, wave
his thanks. Then we forgot the hay and Waterstraw
till he came back in April to start the seasons' circle.

For years, our summer days were marked by waves
of growing hay, and by Darwin Waterstraw,
straight-backed on his tractor, making the circle.

MATISSE'S *ICARUS*

A black silhouette
on deep blue
with yellow stars.
A red circle
on the chest.

The dreamer
backlit
against the sky
flying
toward ecstatic stars,
his red heart
singing?

Or the fallen
body, heart
bursting,
sprawled
in the sea,
the stars,
his light
expiring?

WRITERS' RETREAT

You'd like to think that this could be your life.
While you wander in and out of words,
someone else shops, prepares food, cleans.
You'd like to think that, cared for like this,
the right words would come easily.
And they would be pretty words: velvet,
azure, plumage, rustling like silk onto the page.
In the writers' retreat life, in the lovely room,
overlooking the sweep of shoreline, you'd like to think
there will be no artillery barrage of words that crackle
and burn, no wounded words, no breakage.
But even here, you cannot escape the smoke
of words burning on the other side of the world.
You cannot escape the sniper sitting in your head,
taking aim, waiting for you to move into the crosshairs.

ABOUT THE POET

Lucile Burt is a retired high school English and creative writing teacher. She currently lives in Wellfleet, MA. Inspiration for her poems comes from memory and from observation. The rural landscape of her childhood in upstate New York serves as a backdrop for some poems, while outer Cape Cod, that narrow land surrounded by water, has inspired more recent work. Many years as a teacher provided material about young people and about the classroom. The work of writing poetry, with its careful attention to sound and rhythm, is a kind of meditation that helps her see connections that might otherwise go unnoticed.

ACKNOWLEDGEMENTS

The support and criticism of an on-going poets' group has been invaluable. Most of the poems in this volume have been made better by the wise critiques of members of that group: Susan Webb, Jeanne Washington, Lee Tupman, Leo Thibault, Beebe Pearson, Donna O'Connor, Barry Hellman, and Marjorie Block. Workshops with established poets, including Marge Piercy, Mark Doty, Marie Howe, Billy Collins, and especially Keith Althaus, have helped develop new approaches. Over several decades, many friends and family members have offered encouragement through listening to poems, offering critiques, attending readings, and celebrating successes.

Some poems in this collection were previously published: "Saving the Turtles" and "One Summer" in *Red Rock Review*; "Melissa Quits School" in the anthology *Teaching with Fire*, edited by Parker Palmer and Tom Vander Ark; "Autumn Equinox, Duck Pond" in *The Lunar Calendar* edited by Nancy F. W. Passmore; and "Sleeping at the Beach" in *Tendril*.

This book was typeset by The Poet's Press for The Providence Athenaeum in Calisto with ITC Symbol and Futura titles. Two hundred copies were printed, of which 26 are signed and lettered by the author.

This is the fourteenth title in the Philbrick Poetry Project chapbook series. The previous titles are:

Coats Field by Marjorie Milligan (1999)
The Singed Horizon by Mimi White (2000)
Percussion, Salt & Honey by Nehassaiu deGannes (2001)
What We Planted by Laura Cherry (2002)
AntiGraphi by Linda Voris (2003)
Mr. Gravity's Blue Holiday by Justin Lacour (2004)
Heady Rubbish by Lynn Tudor Deming (2005)
Last Summer by J. F. Connolly (2006)
Toward Anguish by Leslie McGrath (2007)
Chrysalis by John Brush (2008)
Auction by Jennifer E. Whitten (2009)
The Waiting Room by Kathleen M. Kelley (2010)
Workers' Rites by Ellen LaFleche (2011)

Made in the USA
Lexington, KY
25 September 2013